STUDENT WORKBOOK TO ACCOMPANY

ANALYSIS OF TONAL MUSIC
A Schenkerian Approach

Third Edition

STUDENT WORKBOOK TO ACCOMPANY

ANALYSIS OF TONAL MUSIC

A Schenkerian Approach

THIRD EDITION

Allen Cadwallader
Oberlin Conservatory of Music

David Gagné
*Queens College and the Graduate Center,
City University of New York*

New York   Oxford
OXFORD UNIVERSITY PRESS

Oxford University Press, Inc., publishes works that further Oxford University's objective of excellence in research, scholarship, and education.

Oxford   New York
Auckland   Cape Town   Dar es Salaam   Hong Kong   Karachi
Kuala Lumpur   Madrid   Melbourne   Mexico City   Nairobi
New Delhi   Shanghai   Taipei   Toronto

With offices in
Argentina   Austria   Brazil   Chile   Czech Republic   France   Greece
Guatemala   Hungary   Italy   Japan   Poland   Portugal   Singapore
South Korea   Switzerland   Thailand   Turkey   Ukraine   Vietnam

For titles covered by Section 112 of the US Higher Education Opportunity Act, please visit www.oup.com/us/he for the latest information about pricing and alternate formats.Published by Oxford University Press, Inc.

198 Madison Avenue, New York, New York 10016
http://www.oup.com

ISBN 978-0-19-973248-7

Printing number: 9 8 7 6 5 4

Printed in the United States of America
on acid-free paper

CONTENTS

PREFACE

This workbook is designed to accompany *Analysis of Tonal Music: A Schenkerian Approach*, Third Edition, and contains forty-one assignments for introductory courses in Schenkerian analysis. It is designed for students with no previous exposure to Schenkerian analysis, though it can also be used with more advanced students. This edition of the workbook differs from the previous edition in significant ways.

New in This Edition

- We have linked the assignments to examples and discussions in the text, directing students to model their work on specific text analyses. In some cases we recommend certain procedures—for instance, we sometimes suggest students use three structural levels—though instructors should always feel free to alter the instructions to suit the needs of the class. Students will answer questions on the music or on their own staff paper as appropriate.
- To provide instructors with greater flexibility in using the assignments, we have removed the worksheets (the perforated graph paper) and, consequently, all of their notational hints. We do provide hints and suggestions but as part of the instructions, which are now given in narrative form rather than as a list. Instructors, therefore, may choose to ignore the hints, use them as presented, or supplement them with additional hints and suggestions as needed. In this way instructors have much greater freedom in how they incorporate the various compositions into class discussions and use them for homework assignments.
- We have included seventeen new assignments, providing additional practice in structural melody, the imaginary continuo, recognizing harmonic function and class, and distinguishing between "chord" and "harmony" (*Stufe*). *Analysis of Tonal Music* is a text designed for beginners, though it can also be used for more advanced students.
- We have included more assignments for the early chapters, helping reinforce material for students who have had no previous exposure to Schenkerian analysis.

How to Use the Workbook

Instructors should freely adapt the assignments to the needs of their students. For instance, in many assignments we suggest preliminary steps, such as constructing Roman numeral analyses or imaginary continuos. We also pose specific ideas and questions for consideration. These may be considered rhetorical and discussed informally in class, or instructors may wish to make the questions or preliminary analytical steps integral to the assignment and have students answer and hand them in on separate sheets of paper.

Readers will notice that Chapters 1, 6, and 12 are not represented. The reasons for not including assignments for Chapters 1 and 12 should be clear: Chapter 1 is an introduction, and Chapter 12 is devoted primarily to theoretical concerns. In the text, Chapter 6 covers individual techniques of melodic prolongation in restricted contexts. Any assignments focusing on specific techniques would be, in our view, virtually self-evident and without pedagogical value. Furthermore, the various techniques are amply represented in the compositions presented for other chapters.

In this new workbook, it is our intention to provide a kind of annotated anthology that will better serve the needs of both students and instructors, linking the analytical assignments to specific models presented in the text.

Acknowledgments

We would like to express our sincerest thanks to Karen Bottge, who edited and proofread the manuscript with meticulous care, and we extend our appreciation also to Don Giller, who prepared the new scores for this edition and to Kate Ettinger, who assisted in gathering the Urtext editions. We are grateful to Benjamin Levy at Arizona State University and Frank Samarotto at Indiana University for reviewing the manuscript, and we also thank the following reviewers who read the revision plan for this edition: Graham Hunt, University of Texas at Arlington; Anthony Kosar, Westminster Choir College of Rider University; Ciro Scotto, University of South Florida; and Gordon Sly, Michigan State University.

Assignment No. 1   Beethoven, Seven Variations on "God Save the King," WoO 78, Theme and Variation 1 (Chapter 2)

A movement or composition based on a theme and a set of variations clearly exemplifies the role of *repetition* as a fundamental shaping force in music. For beginning studies in Schenkerian analysis, the study of variation procedures also throws into sharp relief the notions of *diminution, melodic fluency*, and *structural melody* (review Chapter 2 for our discussions of these concepts).

First, examine the preexistent melody that Beethoven uses as his theme and compare it to Mozart's theme presented in Example 2.16. In what ways does the theme resemble a cantus firmus and consequently exhibit the properties of melodic fluency? At this stage, it will prove useful to analyze the succession of chords on the score with Roman numerals. The chord in bar 2, on the second part of beat 2, results from passing tones and simply expands V. What other chords have a similar contrapuntal function? In this analysis, do not use Roman numerals for chords that are purely contrapuntal in function.

Now begin your analysis of Variation 1 by identifying, circling, and beaming the tones of the theme on the score; use Example 2.17 as your model. As you might remember from our discussion in Chapter 2, the tones not belonging to the theme are referred to as *diminution*—tones that decorate and embellish the theme. Use letters from the following list to label the function of each tone of diminution:

P = passing tone

N = neighbor note

IN = incomplete neighbor note (or appoggiatura)

CS = consonant or chordal skip

Susp. = suspension

Ant. = anticipation

You might notice that the theme itself contains passing and neighbor notes, which can be considered tones of figuration *on a higher level*. For now, identify only the tones that embellish the underlying theme, the "structural melody" of Variation 1.

In Chapter 2, we discussed (regarding Mozart's composition, Examples 2.16–2.18) what factors other than the preexistent status of the theme "permit" the analyst to circle the tones that make up the structural melody. We suggest that you now ask the same question about Beethoven's variation; use your harmonic analysis of the theme as you consider the question and answer. Notice that, in both the theme and Variation 1, the melody falls to the tonic before rising a fifth to G after the double bar. Also, in Variation 1, the tone E in bars 3–4 is embellished by higher tones (G and F). We can say that these tones are "superimposed" above the main melodic tone, E.

Assignment 1

Assignment 1

Assignment No. 2   Corelli, Variations on "La Folia," Op. 5, No. 12 [Theme (bars 1–16), Variation 5 (bars 81–96), and Adagio (bars 201–216)] (Chapter 3)

"La Folia" is a dance song, at one time associated with wild singing and dancing (the Portuguese translation for *Folia* is "insanity"). The mature form—appearing from about the first part of the seventeenth century—comprises a harmonic pattern supporting a basic melody. Many composers in the seventeenth and eighteenth centuries used this pattern as the basis for variations. The distinction between Corelli's "theme" and Beethoven's folk tune (Assignment No. 1) is that the primary compositional element (the "common denominator" used for subsequent variation) is an explicit succession of chords, not just a single-line melody (which also implies a harmonic underpinning).

This movement is written for violin and a continuo group (Corelli specifies a harpsichord and a low string instrument, as is typical for *basso continuo* performance in the Baroque period). For the first step, realize the figured bass of bars 1–16 on a separate piece of staff paper (some guidelines for realizing figured basses are provided in Chapter 3). Restrict the right hand to simple chords—that is, to triads and seventh chords. In practice, the keyboard player in this variation probably would not add tones of figuration to the upper parts, because doing so would obscure the elaborate bass figuration written specifically for the left hand of the keyboard part.

Now analyze Variation 5 in the same way as Assignment No. 1, except you will now focus on the bass line. Identify, circle, and beam the tones of the structural melody in the bass, and identify the tones of diminution using the symbols outlined in the first assignment. For this part, however, extend the scope of your analysis. In particular, formulate some observations about Corelli's use of *register*. In the first bar of the variation, for instance, you will circle the left-hand D in two registers. What does this observation suggest about the number of *voices* implied in the left hand? How does Corelli's embellishment of the bass line reflect a similar process written for the violin part? The use of contrasting registers can be a valuable compositional resource for composers: Corelli's wide-ranging bass exhibits only a few possibilities for the treatment of register, although they are common and significant for many tonal compositions. Also, compare bar 95 in Variation 5 to bar 15 in the theme. What notable harmonic change has Corelli made in the variation?

In the Adagio (beginning in bar 201), Corelli departs from the original pattern, changing not only the chord succession, but also the structural upper voice. Notice that the upper-voice line is quite "primitive"; it is even more basic than the original line of the theme. Accordingly, many violinists improvise at this juncture, in effect composing a "free" embellishment of the structural melody Corelli provides.

For the final part of this assignment, write out an "improvised" version of the upper-voice line on another sheet of music paper. Don't, however, write haphazardly. Arpeggiations (chordal skips) should conform to the chords specified in the continuo part (realizing the new continuo is an important step). Add passing tones, neighbor notes, and incomplete neighbors sparingly as appropriate. If possible, study Corelli's use of these tones in other variations (the complete score is available in many libraries or online). Always bear in mind that you are fashioning a free composition, using tones of diminution—defined in strict counterpoint—to elaborate a structural melody.

Assignment 2

Assignment 2

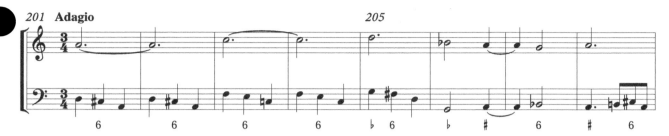

Assignment No. 3   Folk Tune: "Ashgrove" (Chapters 2 and 3)

Unlike the compositions presented in the previous assignments, the Ashgrove melody is not a variation on preexisting material, but a free composition in its own right. (It nonetheless is built on a structural melody.) Your goal is to identify the underlying melodic skeleton based on factors other than the identification of a previously established series of tones.

As we discuss in Chapter 2, in reference to the folk tune "Greensleeves" (Example 2.19), it is often beneficial to construct a chordal reduction when analyzing a single-line melody—a succession of chords implied by the harmonic characteristic of the melody. As we saw in our analysis in the text, the resulting harmonic framework enables you to identify consonant skips (motions between chord tones) and other tones of figuration (*diminution*). We have also seen in Assignment No. 2 that a realization of the figured bass in "La Folia" clarifies the function of the diminution in the embellished lines of the variations.

Begin your analysis of Ashgrove by constructing a simple chordal support, similar to that shown in Example 2.19 (for Greensleeves), using between two and four notes per chord. Bear in mind that V^7 may be part of the harmonic framework; hence, B♭, the 7th of V^7, can serve as a tone of the structural melody. We have provided two staves and suggest beginning the chordal reduction with an F-major triad supporting C as the first "soprano" note; a few other chords are suggested for the cadence.

After you identify the series of chords, circle and beam the broader stepwise line emanating from C in the melody. As you trace the path of the structural melody, you will discover a gap in the line. Considering the stepwise nature of the line to this point, and our suggestion of II^6 for bar 6, what tone would one expect as the continuation of the line in bar 6? Is it present in another voice (of the chordal reduction)? If so, write the tone in the upper staff and enclose it in parentheses.

Interpreting the conclusion of the structural line (bars 1–8) requires careful attention to the functions of tones at the cadence. For instance, does F in bar 7 function similarly to F in bar 8? To answer this question you should review the functions of the sixth and fourth in a cadential $^6_4$ (see our discussion of Example 3.10).

This folk tune comprises three phrases (the first phrase is repeated). Compare the first (bars 1–8) with the second (bars 9–16). How does the skeletal line of bars 9–16 represent a "form" of the line underlying the first phrase?

The structural melody of the second phrase differs from the first in a fundamental way. See if you can determine this significant difference and its ramifications for the entire composition; in other words, what psychological expectation is "thwarted" at the conclusion of the second phrase (but is not at all an issue in the first and third phrases)? Finally, consider these additional questions as you work:

a. How does this melody express vertical triads in the horizontal dimension?
b. What cadences are implied, and where?
c. Are there groups of tones that recur? That is, does the melody contain simple motives (that might or might not involve tones of the structural melodies)?
d. How does the *form* of the folk tune relate to (occur as the result of) the three structural melodies?

Assignment 3

Assignment No. 4   Chopin, Nocturne in F minor, Op. 55, No. 1, bars 1–8 (Chapters 2 and 3)

On another sheet of music paper, begin by creating a block-chord reduction of the left-hand part on a grand staff (treble and bass clefs), including a Roman numeral analysis. What is the form of the structural intermediate harmony? Your instructor will explain the meaning of this chord for this assignment; we will discuss its significance in greater detail in a subsequent chapter.

For the melody, write the tones that belong to the underlying chords. Use broken slurs to show prolonged tones, and solid slurs to show unified motions (as in the examples in Chapter 2).

Next, write a more fundamental melodic line that descends entirely by step from C, considering which tones are supported by structural chords. You will discover a very common usage for V_4^6 (the cadential $_4^6$), which often supports $\hat{3}$ in a descending structural line.

On the score in the workbook, explain the function of the tones not included in your reduction. How are the tones of the main structural descent embellished?

Assignment No. 5   Bellini, "Casta Diva" (from *Norma*), bars 16–23 (Chapters 2 and 3)

Bellini's beautiful melody, in the diminution embellishing the structural melody, is much more complex than that in the folk tune. Consequently, this is the first assignment for which it is beneficial to prepare *two* structural melodies, the second version a derivation ("reduction") of the first. As you work, model your analysis on those of Greensleeves and of Mozart's Theme and Variation in Chapter 2. Your work with Beethoven's Theme and Variation (Assignment No. 1) might also serve as a model for this assignment.

As with previous assignments, first identify and write out the supporting chordal framework, which can be clearly ascertained from the orchestral reduction. Important point: Although the vocal part and accompaniment might be similar, the vocal part is usually considered that part of the tonal framework containing the structural line.

For the first structural melody, after completing the chordal reduction, indicate on the score the tones in the melody belonging to the succession of chords by circling the tones. Some chords may include a passing tone or suspension; in bar 17, for instance, you should include the suspension tone A in your first structural melody, because the first chord of the harmonic framework supports this A in the music. After completing the first structural melody, identify (on a separate piece of music paper) a more basic line (falling and rising) that moves mostly by step, using closed noteheads to indicate the structural tones. The tone B begins and concludes this line.

Finally, explain the function of the tones not included in your reductions. Bear in mind that ornamental tones and structural tones might appear in close proximity. For example, the A in bar 16 becomes a suspension across the bar. Furthermore, the G in the second half of bar 17 is anticipated in the ornamental figure that precedes it.

Assignment 5

(Andante sostenuto assai)

Ca - sta Di - va, ca - sta Di - va che i -nar-

gen - ti   Que - - ste sa - cre, que - ste

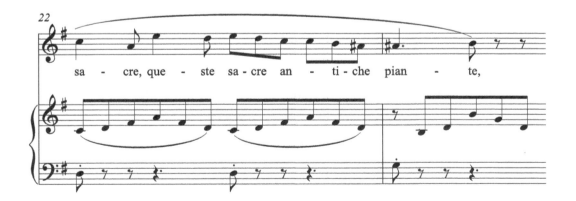

sa - cre, que - ste sa - cre an - ti - che pian - te,

Assignment No. 8   Schubert, Sonata in A minor ("Arpeggione"), bars 10–22 (Chapter 3)

The passage for analysis is the first theme of Schubert's sonata (bars 10–22). Determine the T–Int–D–T of the passage (beginning with the entrance of the solo instrument, bar 10), using the approach of Assignment Nos. 6 and 7 as your create your bass-line analysis. (Note: We will return to the opening of this movement in a later assignment.)

Pay close attention to the motivic role of the neighbor note. This observation should cause you to consider the function of I^6 in bar 17: Does it function as a neighbor chord to the chords in bars 16 and 18? Or, is I^6 the endpoint (the "boundary") of a prolonged tonic *Stufe*? (What does the latter interpretation suggest for the function of $V^6_4-^4_2$ on the third and fourth beats in bar 16?) In any case, you might wish to place I^6 in parentheses in your analysis, for in either analysis it does not by itself represent a structural harmony.

Schubert composes the intermediate area in way that reflects the upper-neighbor motion of this passage; be able to explain the association in words and show it in your graph with some of the symbols and abbreviations used in Chapter 3 (model your analysis on Example 3.14 in the text). The particular form of the intermediate harmony "substitutes" for a more typical II^6, a chromatic transformation we discuss in Chapter 6 (your instructor can explain the subtle difference for this assignment). Play bars 16–22 with a B♮ instead of B♭; notice how the "color" and consequently some of the drama is subdued by substituting the diatonic form of the chord.

Assignment 8

Assignment 8

Assignment No. 9 Schumann, Little Study, bars 1–17 (Chapter 3)

This assignment will give you practice in constructing an imaginary continuo. Model your assignment on Examples 3.18 and 3.19 in the text. (It is reasonable to assume that Schumann's little piece was inspired by Bach's Prelude.) Use a piece of staff paper and make your "realization" (17 bars) look similar to Example 3.19 (the two pieces are very similar in style). Read our suggestions for preparing a chordal reduction before beginning work. You don't need to add Roman numerals to the Schumann, but supply all appropriate figured-bass symbols beneath the chords.

Determine the broader T–Int–D framework of the passage, using Roman numerals sparingly to identify broader harmonic chords and areas. Can the arrival of IV in bar 7 be considered the beginning of the "intermediate area" of the structure? If so, how far does it extend? Consider the following:

a. The leap in the bass and the relationship of the harmonies in bars 13–14.
b. The role of the stepwise bass—the lowest part of the left hand—in bars 7–11.
c. The g♯ in bar 12 intensifies the A-minor harmony in bar 13. In what ways might this II relate to IV in bar 7?
d. The C in the bass (bar 14) is the lowest note of the left hand thus far. Consider how it might relate to a previously stated version of scale-degree $\hat{4}$ in the bass.

The chord in bar 16 is both an extension and an elaboration of the chord in bar 15. In what way would the elimination of bar 16 disturb the rhythmic flow of the music?

Assignment 9

Leise und sehr egal zu spielen.

Assignment No. 10 Chopin, Etude in C major, Op. 10, No. 1, bars 1–9 (Chapter 3)

Chopin's Etude is considerably more difficult than Schumann's "Little Study" and Bach's C-major Prelude (Example 3.18). Nevertheless, despite the obvious stylistic and performance differences, the reduction of the Chopin will show the similarities to the Bach Prelude. Your imaginary continuo realization of bars 1–8 will reveal the common characteristics and in particular the similarities between their structural melodies. (Could Chopin have been thinking of Bach's Prelude when composing his Etude?)

Prepare an imaginary continuo realization (bars 1–8), similar to the one constructed for Assignment No. 9. Use four or five voices in the right hand and one (representing the bass) in the left. Because Chopin's use of register is so free and complex, we suggest that you use e^2 as the top note (right hand) for the first chord of the imaginary continuo. (Notice the accents that highlight this tone in bars 1 and 2.)

Assignment 10

Assignment No. 11 Corelli, Op. 4, No. 5, Corrente (Chapter 3)

In Chapter 3, we use Bach's figured-bass chorale "Ihr Gestirn, ihr hohen Lüfte" to illustrate specific techniques of harmonic prolongation, key areas (*Stufen*) that span larger contexts, and typical harmonic characteristics of the minor mode. For Corelli's composition (which is similar to Bach's in its large-scale layout), create an analysis that resembles Example 3.16. Notice that the Corrente is "rounded," beginning in bar 22, a feature that we will discuss in Chapter 9; this observation will facilitate your analysis.

The example in the book uses two levels of Roman numerals. On the upper level, use Roman numerals (as in Example 3.16) to show local progressions and typical prolongations (review, for instance, bars 3 and 14 in Example 3.16). In the Corelli, bars 1–3 can be represented simply as I–IV^6–V in A minor, a local Phrygian cadential progression. In bars 9 and 10, use IV–V–I to indicate the cadence in C major. Hint: Corelli uses many $^6_3$ chords, so Roman numerals are not always applicable, but C major "begins to develop" in bars 5 and 6. What other local "keys" occur in the Corrente? Identify each key as it occurs, and clearly indicate the return to the tonic.

On the lower level, use Roman numerals sparingly (as in the text example) to indicate only broader harmonies (*Stufen*). Be sure to label each structural harmony with T, Int, or D. Finally, compare the compositions, noting particularly how each composer treats the restatement of the final, structural tonic.

Assignment 11

Assignment No. 15 Bach, Harpsichord Concerto (after Marcello), BWV 974, II, bars 1–15 (Chapter 4)

This assignment should be completed in a manner similar to that specified for Assignment No. 14 (also using Examples 4.13 and 4.17 as models from the text). First prepare a block-chord reduction with figured-bass symbols. The specific figured-bass symbols for bars 6, 8, and 10 depend on which tones you interpret (in the diminution of the right hand) as the "top" notes of the underlying chords.

On a separate piece of staff paper, complete the three-voice setting of the two linear intervallic patterns. The first pattern begins in bar 4 and the second in bar 11. Show with numbers (between the staves) the pattern of the outer voices and add figured-bass symbols beneath the staff. Begin your analysis of the linear intervallic pattern (and associated linear progression) that begins in bar 4; for the imaginary-continuo chord, use a D-minor tonic with two "soprano" notes: f^2 followed by a^2 (a small skip; the F is the resolution of G—in the lower register—from the previous bar).

The first linear intervallic pattern (bars 4–11) is accompanied by a linear progression (as is usually the case). Notice that the superposition of C in bar 4 adds a seventh that is then echoed by the seventh chords in bars 6, 8, and 10. Use a slur to show the horizontalized interval of the underlying *Stufe* prolonged by the repeated pattern of intervals (refer to Example 4.15). Be sure to label the linear progressions (3-prg, 4-prg, etc.) and be able to explain *precisely* why it is appropriate to group the series of tones you find as defining the particular linear progression.

Assignment 15

Assignment No. 16 Bach, Prelude in G minor from "English" Suite No. 3, BWV 808, bars 1–33 (Chapter 4)

Bach wrote the Prelude to his third "English" suite in the manner of a Baroque concerto. The passage presented here, bars 1–33, is the concerto movement's *ritornello*, which exhibits two closely related sequences. The first sequence (and associated linear intervallic pattern) descends in bars 8–14; it is repeated in varied form in bars 15–21. The second sequence (bars 23–27) rises and, in contrast to the first, is more chromatic in nature.

Make an imaginary continuo reduction of the sequential passages (bars 8–14 and 23–27). Be sure to indicate the numbers for the outer-voice intervallic patterns (such as 7–10, 7–10). This should bring the linear progressions and linear intervallic patterns into sharp relief.

Label the linear progressions that accompany these outer-voice intervallic patterns (use Examples 4.15–4.18 in the text as models).

Include a few Roman numerals only for the *Stufen,* and discuss how these sequences relate to the harmonic framework—that is, how the sequences connect the *Stufen.*

Assignment 16

Assignment No. 21   Schubert, Sonata in A minor ("Arpeggione"), bars 1–22 (Chapter 7)

In Assignment No. 8, you analyzed the bass-line structure of Schubert's first theme. Now complete the analysis: this time, however, include the piano introduction in your graphic analysis and complete the assignment in three levels, using Example 7.20 as your model.

Schubert uses an upper-neighbor figure as a prominent motive. How does it recur throughout this passage?

In bar 16, what is the initial main tone in the upper voice, and how does it fit into Schenker's conception of tonal structure? Review specific techniques of melodic prolongation in Chapter 6 to help you with this question.

Assignment 21

Assignment 21

Assignment No. 22   Beethoven, Piano Sonata, Op. 27, No. 1 ("Moonlight"), III, bars 116–137 (Chapter 7)

This passage is the second theme (recapitulation) of the finale from Beethoven's "Moonlight" sonata, a harmonically closed single phrase in C# minor (consider G# as $\hat{5}$ of the *Urlinie* of this passage). Use the same approach as for Assignment Nos. 20 and 21. Use Example 7.30 as your model (the passage analyzed there is also the second theme of a Beethoven Piano Sonata, but as it occurs in the exposition).

Very often the recognition of formal sections can help you make decisions regarding the underlying tonal structure. This phrase is an example of a sentence, which is described in Chapter 7. The first basic idea of the presentation spans bars 116–119, the second basic idea bars 120–123. At this point, a harmonic *elision* occurs at the beginning of the continuation part of the sentence (bars 124–137; review our discussion of an elision in Example 7.11). Consider, in bars 124–127 of the continuation, that both the upper and lower voices simultaneously exhibit linear progressions (the first tone of the progression in the bass is elided).

The main techniques of melodic prolongation applying to G# (beginning in bar 116) are fairly straightforward (the two basic ideas of the sentence differ essentially with respect to register). For the continuation, including the drive to the cadence, consider first whether the descent in the upper voice (bars 123–127) represents the descent of the *Urlinie*. If not, what technique does the descent represent?

Now consider the role of the dramatic intermediate harmony, the deceptive resolution to VI (bar 132), and Beethoven's subsequent "second attempt" to achieve closure in bar 137. The trill in bar 131, although it appears before the second drive to the cadence, will help you to make specific decisions about the ultimate close of the *Urlinie*. For instance, considering that bars 131 and 136 occur at similar places in the harmonic structure (notice in bar 136 the register change, the *leap* to low G#), what technique occurs on the third beat of bar 136?

Assignment 22

Assignment 22

Assignment No. 24 Schumann, *Liederkreis*, Op. 24, "Morgens steh' ich auf" (Chapter 8)

Reflecting our presentation of Schubert's song in Chapter 8 of the text, we suggest you begin by studying the poem. Note its mood and character, and identify any words or phrases that might "suggest" text painting by the composer. Hint: The juxtaposition of day and night represents one possibility.

For this piece, focus first on the bass structure and identify the brief tonicizations between the tonic and V in bar 35 (the song is quite short and begins and ends with a prelude and a postlude). For instance, how do F♯ minor and E minor function in the middleground bass-line structure? Hint: The G-major chord in bar 26 begins a prolongation of the subdominant.

As we also mentioned in the text, the vocal part is usually associated with the melodic structure and, ultimately, the *Urlinie*; notice, however, how bars 1–4 of the piano part prefigure the opening bars of the vocal part. How does the chromaticism in the later part of the vocal line reflect the sentiments of the poem (the ideas and feelings of the protagonist)? Finally, how does the diminution in bars 43–45 (the right hand of the piano part) recall features of the structural melody in the voice over the course of the entire song?

Assignment 24

Assignment 24

hal - ben Schlum - mer, träu - mend wand - le ich bei Tag.

Assignment No. 25 Handel, Theme and Variations in B♭ major, Aria (Chapter 9)

Handel's Aria can be understood as a binary form, similar in type to the ones presented in the first part of Chapter 9. Use Example 9.2 as the model for your graphic analysis (sometimes two levels might suffice—surface/foreground and middleground). The *Urlinie* can be read from either 3̂ or 5̂. One interpretation is not necessarily better than the other, but the relationship between structure and form will differ based on different readings. A point for consideration: Schenker published an analysis of this little piece (we won't divulge his starting point for the *Urlinie*). Your instructor might decide to show you his or her reading after you prepare your own, presenting you with an opportunity to examine aspects of Schenker's analytical thinking.

In your analysis, be especially sensitive to the role of the upper neighbor E♭ in the top voice, which occurs as both a *complete* and an *incomplete* upper neighbor throughout the piece. There are subtle but important distinctions between these contrapuntal formations, and your graph should clearly differentiate their functions in the upper voice.

Prepare two graphs for the Aria, one from 3̂, the other from 5̂. Be able to explain in words and symbols the differences between the foreground and middleground levels of the upper voice. In your reading from 5̂, consider that E♭ can be the "main" tone over A in the bass (bar 6). If so, what are the contrapuntal implications for the E♭ and the following F?

Based on your reading, sketch a structural synopsis (the final level) for the first level of the middleground. A structural synopsis is essentially a deep middleground graph: Use Example 9.4 as an example. Finally, describe (in words) the relationships between form and structure in each of your two readings. Remember, form and structure are related aspects of tonal compositions, but they are not synonymous; review our summary of Schenker's ideas at the beginning of Part 2 of the text.

Assignment No. 26 Handel, Minuet in F major, HWV 516a (Chapter 9)

Use the same approach and instructions as for Assignment No. 25. First, identify the cadences and modulations on the score. Hint: Consider bar 6 as the beginning of a tonicized C-major area.

As you work consider two interpretations for the beginning of the B section. The first involves a return to structural tonic harmony in bar 9; the second regards the passage after the double bar as a prolongation (until bar 23) of the dominant in bar 8. How might the foreground linear motion in the upper voice (bars 9–13) help you to choose between these possibilities?

Another consideration: Does an interruption divide the structure (compare with Example 9.8)? What reasons can you articulate for and against a reading that includes this technique? Hint: The tone a^2 is implied in bar 16 and restated literally in bar 17. Are the preceding occurrences of this tone related at the same structural level?

Handel establishes D minor in bars 14–16. What are the contrapuntal implications of this "key" at the middleground if you consider F major in bar 9 as a return to structural tonic harmony?

Finally, as with the preceding assignment, discuss aspects of form and structure in this Minuet.

Assignment 26

Assignment No. 27 Bach (Anon.), Menuet in D minor, BWV Anhang 132 (Chapter 9)

Use the same approach and instructions as for Assignment No. 25, and compare this assignment with Example 9.1. First, identify the type of binary form, label the cadences, and determine the number of phrases. Determining the first tone of the *Urlinie* can be challenging in this composition; scale-degrees $\hat{3}$, $\hat{5}$, and $\hat{1}$ appear in close proximity in bar 1. Hint: What tone seems to be *implied* in bar 4 (consider the voice leading of the previous measure)? For the modulation, consider that III begins to "develop" by the conclusion of bar 5; the Roman numerals of the imaginary continuo (third beat of bar 5 to the downbeat of bar 6) are V^4_2–I^6 in the key of F major.

In the B section, the upper voice clearly begins on a^2, which initiates a descending linear progression; what tone is the endpoint of the progression? Also, the V in bar 12 is a triad; the V in bar 14, on the other hand, is a V^7, supporting g^2. These observations should help you identify the function of the linear progression beginning in bar 9, and, consequently, the longer-range association from a^2.

Don't forget to consider idiosyncratic motivic features and repetitions; compare, for instance, the upper voice in bars 3 and 14, and the bass in bar 12 with the upper voice in bar 13. Finally, as with previous assignments for Chapter 9, discuss the distinction between form and structure in this Menuet.

Assignment No. 28 Mozart, Piano Sonata, K. 547a, III (Thema) (Chapter 9)

Mozart's little binary form presents some difficulties in analyzing the upper voice, particularly in bars 1–8; notice the jagged, broken motions of the right hand. Certainly we have seen such wide-ranging separated lines before and have discovered that melodically fluent, stepwise lines can underlie a complex interplay of registers. (This is one passage for which an imaginary continuo realization would prove very useful. Compare this exercise with Examples 9.5 and 9.6.) Hint: What does the motion G–G♯ (bars 1–2, different registers) suggest for the main tone over tonic harmony in bar 2? Note also the double voice exchange in bar 3.

The bass-line harmonic structure of the first phrase is also tricky. Hint: Consider that F♯, which begins the second phrase, is related over a longer span to the tonic F at the beginning of the first phrase. This reading will suggest at least two different analytical interpretations for consideration:

a. Is the V in bar 4 back relating, so that the large-scale half-step motion F (bar 1) to F♯ (anacrusis to the second phrase) "overrides" the V at the half cadence in bar 4?

b. Or, does the appearance of F♯ in bar 4 simply represent an elision, taking the place of an understood F natural (of a root-position tonic)?

The B section is less complex (at least in terms of register), so we will offer only a few remarks. The g^2 in bar 9 appears to "pop up" suddenly. Perhaps it reestablishes the "real" upper voice? If such is the case, then from what tone does g^2 follow over a longer span? And does g^2 (it is repeated) lead to F or A in bars 12–14? The answer to this question might not be as obvious as it first appears.

Important point: The cadences in bars 7–8 and 15–16 are identical and form a kind of musical "rhyme" in the form of the composition. But the two I^6 chords that begin each cadence pattern *do not represent a return to structural tonic harmony.* Hint: The voice exchanges in bars 7 and 15 (between outer voices) should help you evaluate the harmonic context. Your instructor can shed additional light on this very common bass motion, which occurs often at cadences in Baroque and Classical compositions. As always, discuss the relationship between form and structure; because, however, the next assignment introduces other considerations, we will be more specific and suggest you consider the "nature" of the *Urlinie* and how it relates to the two-part *form.*

Assignment 28

Assignment No. 29 Chopin, Prelude in G major, Op. 28, No. 3 (Chapters 7 and 9)

From a formal/structural perspective, Chopin's G-major Prelude stands midway between the binary forms already examined and those that remain for Chapter 9. In fact, you will notice that some of the shorter passages in Chapter 7 of the text reflect the period structure of the Prelude. Hence you can use graphs from both Chapter 7 (Examples 7.16 and 7.17) and Chapter 9 (see, in particular, Example 9.14) as your guides for this analysis.

First, identify the cadences and number of phrases. For the first phrase, examine *carefully* the opening figuration in the left hand (it is an introduction to the piece). There is more to this accompaniment than appears at first glance; you should keep its characteristics in mind as you analyze the remainder of the Prelude.

The second phrase, although beginning similarly to the first, quickly veers off and introduces new material. Notice in particular the harmony prolonged from bars 18–23 (which does not appear in the first phrase). Hint: This harmony and a tone it supports are "motivated" by a feature—an appoggiatura—in the left hand's opening flourish. Another hint is that by the conclusion of the prolongation (bar 23), the specific Roman numeral is different from that in bar 18 (although both represent the same intermediate *Stufe*).

We have suggested an association between the opening left-hand diminution and the "new" material in the second phrase. But see if you can also discover how this diminution foreshadows (perhaps more tangibly) the technique that applies to the *Urlinie* in the first phrase. Remember that a consideration of this type pertains to *analysis* (as opposed to the more general idea of theory). Although theory and analysis are interrelated, and work interactively in a spiral of understanding (sometimes referred to as the "hermeneutic circle"), the act of analysis seeks to reveal the special idiosyncratic features that mark a composition as a unique work of art.

Assignment 29

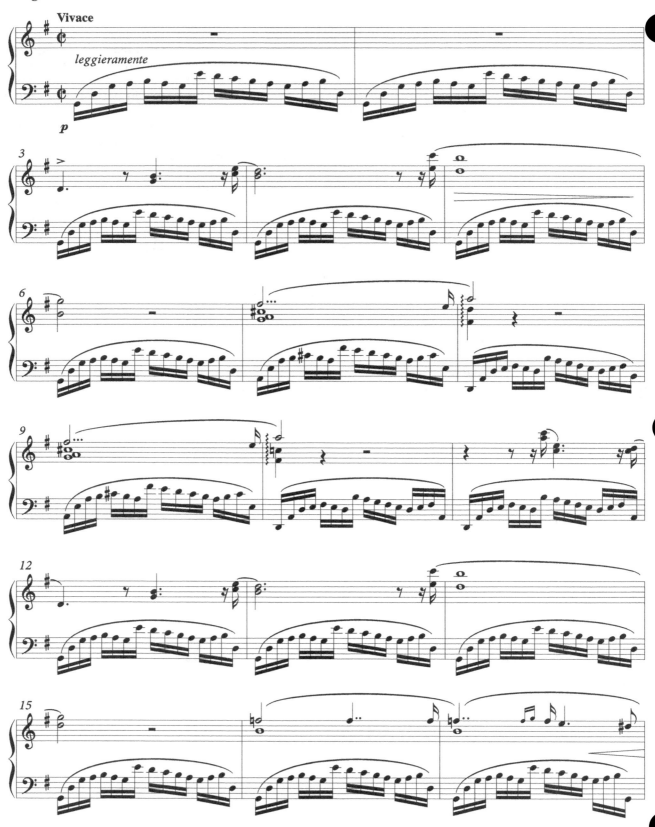

Assignment 29

Assignment No. 30   Schumann, *Dichterliebe*, "Ich will meine Seele tauchen" (Chapters 8 and 9)

This composition shares structural features with Chopin's Prelude in the previous assignment; use the instructions and approach for that assignment in your analysis of Schumann's song. Prepare a graphic analysis (two or three levels) and use Example 8.6 as your model. Important: Because this is a song, study the words before analyzing the music, determining any words or phrases that Schumann might earmark for "text painting."

Notice that the music does not begin with tonic harmony; review our discussion of *auxiliary cadences* in Chapter 9 (pp. 256–259). As you work you will discover another auxiliary cadence that establishes the first of two intermediate chords; use similar graphic notation for both auxiliary cadences.

Bar 9 begins the consequent phrase (the second branch of the divided fundamental structure). In principle, your graph of bars 9–16 will be essentially the same as for the antecedent phrase. Be sure, however, to consider carefully any changes (no matter how slight), particularly those occurring at the perfect authentic cadence in bars 15–16.

74

Assignment 30

Leise.

Ich will mei - ne See - le tau - - chen in den

Kelch der Li - lie hin - ein, die Li - lie soll klin - gend

han - chen ein Lied von der Lieb - sten mein. Das

Assignment 30

Lied soll schau - ern und be - ben wie der kass von ih - rem

Mund,' den sie mir einst___ ge - ge - ben in

wun - der - bar süs - ser Stund'!

Assignment 30

Assignment No. 31 Beethoven, Bagatelle, Op. 119, No. 9 (Chapter 9)

This little piece is a so-called rounded binary form (review our discussion of form and structure at the beginning of Part 2 in the text). As a first step, identify and label all of the cadences on the score. Your goal is to prepare a graphic analysis that depicts two or three structural levels; use Examples 9.13 and 9.14 as your models.

The piece incorporates two registers in the right hand. What is the specific technique of melodic prolongation that links the middle to the higher register in the opening bars? Review also Example 6.12 in the text. In several measures, a tone of the *Urlinie* is chromatically inflected. Where does its "♮" form appear? What melodic technique (discussed in the text) does this tone represent? Hint: In bar 3, the main tone is *not* C (think of the imaginary-continuo chord implied by the left hand). Important: Notice that the first part concludes in the tonic, not on V as in Chopin's G-major Prelude.

The next part (after the double bar) is a separate B section that concludes on V (note the fermata that marks the section's conclusion). Consider also, in the B section, a prominent voice-leading motion in the upper voice, from B to C (twice). Also, consider the accompanying upward motions to e³; what is the specific technique of melodic prolongation these high points represent?

Finally, beginning in bar 13, the opening part is repeated *exactly* (an A² section). Three interruptions occur in this piece, but only one resides at a deep middleground level. Consider this aspect when notating the various *Urlinie* patterns. In other words, distinguish carefully between those tones requiring filled-in noteheads and higher ranking pitches represented by open noteheads. In effect, the technique of interruption leads to an "out-of-phase" characteristic between the parts of the form and the parts of the structure (often typical of a rounded binary). Be sure you can explain the complex interaction of form and structure in words and depict it graphically in your sketch.

Assignment 31

Vivace moderato

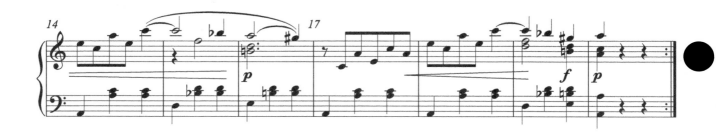

Assignment No. 32 Haydn, String Quartet, Op. 74, No. 3, II, bars 1–22 (Chapter 9)

This section of Haydn's movement (bars 1–22) is a binary form closed in the tonic. (In a later assignment, you will analyze the complete movement as a ternary form.) Analyze this passage in the same manner as that for Examples 9.13 and 9.14 (rounded binary).

Some hints for the passage: What is the traditional name of the chord in bar 8? How does it introduce and prepare the next tone of the *Urlinie*? In bar 12, consider the Roman numeral (in B major) of the chord on beats 3–4. Where does one expect it to resolve (and where is that expectation fulfilled)? An *unfolded* pair of intervals occurs in the upper and lower voices of bar 13 (review this technique in Chapter 6). The E-major chords in that bar do not represent structural tonic harmony.

A consideration pertaining to analysis: How are the chords in bars 8 and 12 (beats 1–2) related? (The first is marked *fortissimo*, the second *pianissimo*.) Finally, consider Haydn's use of middle and high registers in the upper voice and comment on how register is used in a compositional sense (this aspect will become more fully apparent when you analyze the complete movement in a later assignment).

Assignment 32

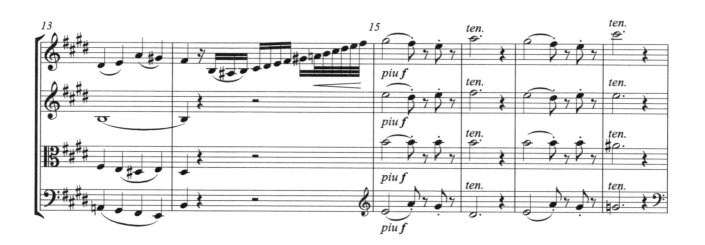

Assignment 32

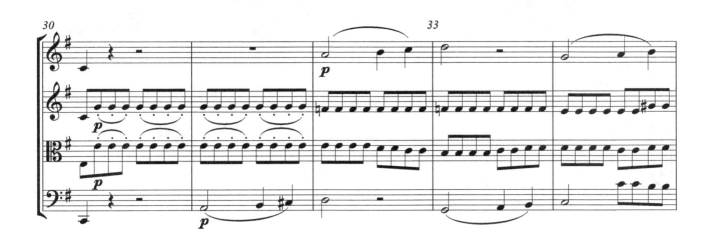

Assignment 32

Assignment 32

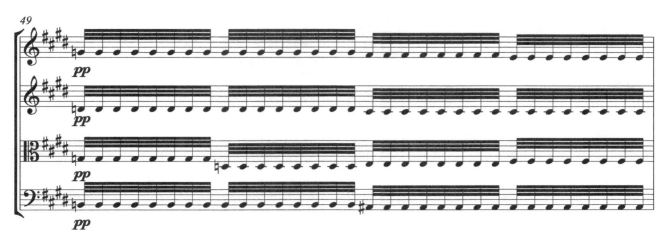

Assignment 32

Assignment 32

Assignment No. 33 Haydn, String Quartet, Op. 64, No. 5, II, bars 1–34 (Chapter 9)

This passage is similar to that from Haydn's String Quartet presented in the previous assignment; use the same approach and models in Chapter 9 in analyzing this rounded binary form.

Some points and hints for consideration: A subdominant chord is introduced in bar 5 and can be prolonged and transformed for more than two bars (in this regard, consider a connection between D in the bass and a chromatic transformation of D in bar 7).

A C$^\sharp$ appears over the chord in bar 13, which is V$^4_2$ in the "new" key. What ramification does this observation hold for the function of C$^\sharp$ in the upper voice (review in particular Example 9.12)? From a broader perspective, what technique underlies the "emergence" of E major in bars 13–16?

The little B section runs from bars 17–22. Consider that at least part of the cello's line belongs to a "tenor voice," above a sustained (but silent) bass note. Hint: The notion of a bass/tenor "space" is suggested previously by the octave Es in bar 16. In this reading, regard the structural bass as literally resuming in bar 21.

The major change in the A^2 section occurs in bars 29–31; we regard the IV chords in bars 27 and 31 as connected. What, then, are some possible interpretations for bars 28–31, the new material of the section? Finally, comment on the primary difference between the cadence of the A^1 section and that of the A^2 section.

Assignment 33

Assignment 33

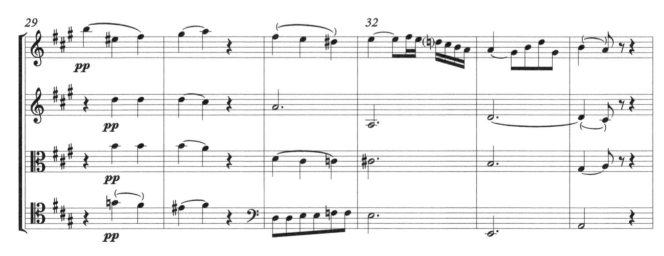

Assignment No. 34 Mozart, Clarinet Quintet, K. 581, III (Trio I) (Chapter 9)

This piece—a complete Trio—is the final binary presented for Chapter 9. Hint: This composition is traditionally referred to as a rounded binary, but it also comes very close to exhibiting the characteristics of a little *sonata* form (more on this in a later assignment). Use Examples 9.12–9.14 as your guides.

Some points and hints for consideration: The first violin (in the A^1 section) continually moves above the *Urlinie*. How do you explain the tones and motions in the higher register *not* belonging to the *Urlinie* proper? How is the intermediate harmony of C major expanded (beginning in bar 11)? The answer should help you determine the nature of Mozart's asymmetrical groups of measures: the first group is from bars 1–7, the second (counting bar 7 also as a beginning measure) from bars 7–16 (7 + 10).

Mozart recomposes certain portions of the A^2 section so that the entire section is in the home tonic (one reason why it approaches a sonata in construction). Identify the place in the corresponding spot in the A^1 section where Mozart makes the change in the A^2 section. For instance, Mozart uses a Neapolitan sixth chord as the intermediate harmony in the A^2 section (compare to II^6 in the A^1 section). Can you posit a reason why he chooses to use the Neapolitan sixth in bars 36–39 instead of II^6 in A minor (which would result from a literal transposition down a fifth of bars 11–14 from the A^1 section)?

Another important consideration: The first choice for the first tone of the *Urlinie* is perhaps e^2 of the anacrusis. Can you think of reasons why c^2 in bar 4 might also be considered a possibility?

Assignment 34

Assignment 34

Assignment 34

M. D. C. senza replica

Assignment No. 35 Haydn, String Quartet, Op. 74, No. 3, II (B section and completion of movement) (Chapter 10)

For this assignment, you will analyze the B section of the Haydn movement you began in Assignment No. 32. As you discovered, however, considered as a unit closed in the tonic, the A^1 section is a binary form. Form in tonal music—like harmony and counterpoint—is hierarchical. Hence a higher level of form *embraces* the binary forms of the flanking A sections (such pieces are sometimes referred to as "composite" forms).

Your goal is to consider how Haydn integrates a section in E minor into an E-major *Ursatz*. Examples 10.1 through 10.6 present clear instances of "form within form," as well as illustrating how sections in different modes function in a unified *Ursatz*. Review our discussion of Schenker's conception of mixture in Chapter 6.

One approach to the analysis of composite forms is to treat each autonomous section as a small, but complete composition (the approach underlying the passages examined in Chapter 7); then combine them to see how the relate compositionally. In other words, analyze the B section without reference to your previous analysis, and then consider how it functions in relation to the A^1 and A^2 sections.

How does C major—the primary tonicization of the B section—relate to the tonic of E minor and ahead to the V that concludes the B section? In short, what is the T–Int–D structure underlying the A^1 and B sections? Comment on the recomposition Haydn makes for the A^2 section and on the coda that follows it and portray it graphically. Can you discover (in the very brief coda, bars 60–64) the rather literal motivic recollections drawn from the A and B sections?

Assignment 35

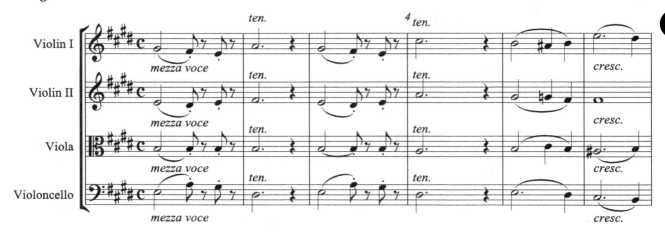

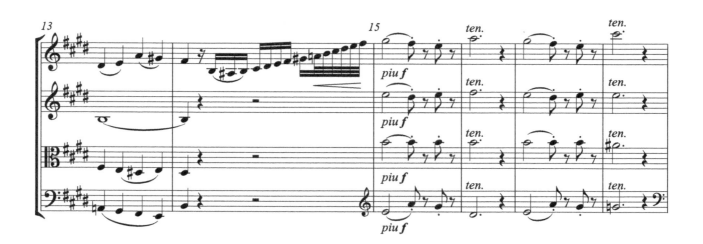

Assignment 35

Assignment 35

Assignment 35

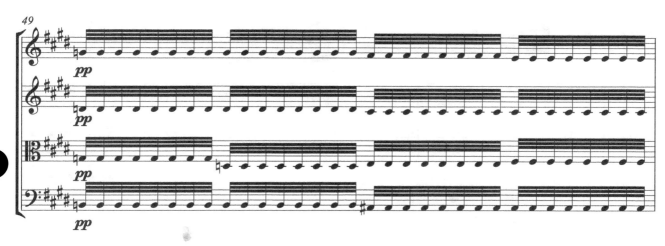

Assignment 35

Assignment 35

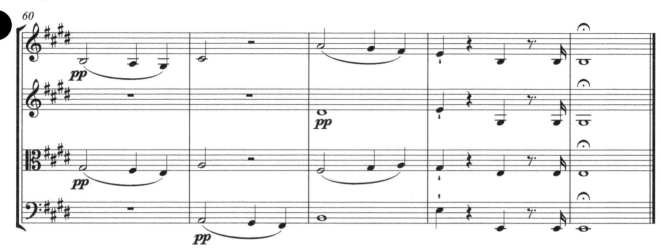

Assignment No. 36 Brahms, Intermezzo, Op. 118, No. 2, B section (bars 49–73) (Chapter 10)

The B section of Brahms's Intermezzo is a separate formal section (a ternary design) closed in the key of F♯ minor. Analyze this section using Example 10.9 as your guide. Brahms uses a recurring "basic" motive (beginning in the upper voice of bar 49) throughout this section, a succession of tones that decorates the primary tone of the section's *Urlinie*. Comment on the various ways in which he repeats and expands this motive. In particular, look for the motive recurring *imitatively* (almost canonically). Also, be cognizant of the compound melodies in both the right and left hands.

Some hints and questions for consideration: As a first step, identify all the phrases and cadences. The c♯2 on the downbeat of bar 50 is a passing tone, not a resumption of the primary tone of the *Urlinie*. In the bass, the F♯s in bars 53–54 are related, supporting a 5–6 shift over tonic harmony. This procedure is quite common in moving from I to V (see Example 12.8b).

In the b section, bars 57–64, what ramification does the *retention* of the key of F♯ (although a different mode) have for the motivic *unification* of the large B section? (As in Chapter 10, note the use of lowercase letters to identify formal patterns *within* the large sections of the Intermezzo.) Comment on an *Urlinie* descent in the F♯-major passage (compare to Assignment No. 4, Chopin's Nocturne in F minor). Describe the ways in which Brahms recomposes the a2 section (bars 65–73). Note that the climax of the B section occurs in bar 69. What aspects contribute to the perception of "climax," and what structural feature of the *Urlinie* is thereby emphasized?

Assignment 36

Assignment 36

Assignment No. 37 Beethoven, Piano Sonata, Op. 7, II (Chapter 10)

This assignment, like the Haydn movement in Assignment Nos. 32 and 35, is a composite ternary form. (See also Example 10.26 in the textbook, which is also a ternary form.) For the A^1 section: A prolonged V (bars 10–14) follows the tonic area. What structural tone (of the *Urlinie*) is prolonged over the V? What form-producing technique precedes the return of the main theme in bar 15? Notice the bass figure A–A♭–G in bars 13–14. As you analyze, notice the similar chromatic motions that can recur in other sections and at different structural levels. Finally, one expects tonic harmony in bar 20. What occurs instead? How does the motion in bars 20–23 relate to the cadential motion in bars 17–19?

For the B section: The passage begins in A♭ major. Consider the large-scale harmonic function of this *Stufe* in relation to the structural V in bar 37. This goal is intensified and preceded by a chromatic chord that often signals the conclusion or *boundary* of a prolongational span (review our discussion of prolongational spans in the text). The boundary relates to the A♭-major chord at the beginning of the section (bar 25); together they form a harmonic "frame" (for prolongation). Closer to the foreground, the bass moves through various "waypoints" (beginning on A♭) in an arpeggiation that leads to D♭ major in bar 33, a temporary goal highlighted by a repetition of the main theme of the B section. The bass then initiates a rising linear progression; consider the goal of this motion as a resumption of the beginning chord of the section.

Conclusion: Because the A^2 section is a virtual repetition of the A^1 section, we present only a few comments about the coda. The top voice begins on g^2, which initiates a rising linear progression supported by a motion from I to V. What structural tone does this progression recall? Beethoven uses the motion A♭–G as a "character" throughout the piece, a motive recurring (in various guises) in the tonal drama of the movement. As you analyze the coda, consider the versions of this motive to those in the A^1 and B sections. For instance, what is the relationship of the bass in bars 13–14 to the *large-scale bass of the B section*, and, subsequently, to bars 82–83 in the coda?

Assignment 37

Largo, con gran espressione

Assignment 37

Assignment 37

Assignment 37

Assignment No. 38 Brahms, Intermezzo in A minor, Op. 76, No. 7 (Chapter 10)

By this time, you have gained considerable experience making graphs and applying Schenker's approach to analysis. In the remaining assignments, therefore, we limit our comments to suggesting specific text models and providing hints by formal section (sometimes we will present the hints in the form of rhetorical questions).

See Examples 10.26–10.31 in relation to this piece. Does the A^1 section begin at the very beginning of the piece or in the anacrusis to bar 9? Likewise, the opening bars are repeated at the conclusion of the Intermezzo; hence is this concluding passage a coda or an integral part of the A^2 section? (A composition with a "prelude" and "postlude" is certainly a possibility.) What specific technique does Brahms use to establish C major (III) by the double bar?

To evaluate the first part of the B section, consider that A^1 concludes (bar 16) with C in the bass and E in the upper voice. The chromatic linear motions (in the outer voices) at the beginning of the B section follow from these points of departure. Notice also the two-bar "voice exchanges" between soprano and bass in bars 17–18 and 19–20. Hint: What harmony is prolonged by these procedures? Finally, consider the chord succession leading away from III and toward V of A minor (bars 21–24) as II^7–V–I in the key of E.

Considering the purposeful motions reestablishing A minor in bars 24–27, you might read a return to structural tonic harmony here, a plausible interpretation that would signal an A^2 section. Another, more esoteric reading is also possible (both work with the imaginary continuo). Consider the length and emphasis of the subdominant *Stufe* beginning in bar 28. It might be possible to posit that D minor develops from the previous C-major *Stufen* (III) at the double bar; in this situation, a structural V (at the first level of the middleground) does not appear in bars 23–26. In both situations—including others you might arrive at independently—consider whether an interruption divides the structure of this Intermezzo. If an interruption is not present, explain from a Schenkerian perspective how a three-part form develops within an undivided *Urlinie*.

Assignment 38

Assignment 38

Assignment 38

Assignment No. 39 Mozart, Piano Sonata, K. 279, Andante (Chapter 11)

The second movement of Mozart's Piano Sonata, K. 279, is in sonata form. Because of its breadth, we present comments and points for consideration in three sections, corresponding to the exposition, development, and recapitulation. Use Examples 11.5ff. as your guides; consult also the general patterns on the sonata principle in Chapter 12.

For the exposition: Determine the main cadences, key areas, and subsections. At what point does Mozart write a perfect authentic cadence in the new key area, which marks the beginning of the closing section? How is the cadence avoided and postponed? In bars 10–17, scale-degree $\hat{2}$ of the *Urlinie* is prolonged with a fifth-progression; why can this line *not* be the *Urlinie* of the C-major area? A perfect authentic cadence occurs in bars 25–26, accompanied by one of Mozart's characteristic trills, signaling the structural close of the exposition. Address how Mozart expands the second fifth-progression $\hat{5}$–$\hat{1}$ in C major.

For the development: The prolongation of $\hat{2}$ over V is the most characteristic plan for major-mode development sections. This does not mean, however, that V is always present; secondary motions, often in different keys, might serve to prolong the underlying V. The V^7 in bars 41–42 is the boundary of the dominant prolongation and the chord that prepares the tonic of the recapitulation. How, for instance, might one relate the A-major triads (V of D minor) to the C-major chord at the beginning of the development section? In this section, I^6 (in D minor) is prominent, emphasized through the bass motions G-F in bars 33 and 35. (Note that the *root-position* D-minor chord is played softly, which suggests a lower-ranking status.) This observation should help you to organize the lower-level motions of the development section.

For the recapitulation: Because of the obvious repetitions from the exposition, you should have no trouble sketching the recapitulation. Consider that the second part of the exposition—the area in V (C major)—recurs transposed down a fifth into the tonic. In other words, all motions not heard initially in the tonic recur in F major, including the second *Urlinie* and its elaborations. From a broader perspective, how must the transposition of the secondary fifth-progression be interpreted in terms of the *Ursatz*?

Assignment 39

Assignment 39

Assignment 39

Assignment 39

Assignment No. 40 Clementi, Sonatina, Op. 36, No. 3, I (Chapter 11)

Clementi's movement is a "little" sonata, exhibiting techniques on a small scale that apply to more extended sonata movements. As with other sonata assignments, it will be useful to consult the analysis of Mozart's "Haffner" Symphony in the text.

For the exposition: Analyze the exposition in sections, bars 1–12 (C major), and bars 13–26 (G major). Consider each as a lower-level *Ursatz* parallelism. Before beginning to sketch, be able to explain Schenker's principle of the *transference of the forms of the fundamental structure to individual harmonies*. Compare with the dominant area in Examples 11.7 and 11.8 Make a preliminary analysis showing *two* lower-level fundamental structures, one in C major and the other in G major. Consider the fundamental line of the G-major area as an "offshoot"—a secondary linear progression—of the main *Urlinie* of the exposition. In the C-major section, consider the melodic function of A (often expressed as a^2); this tone occurs as part of the "$\hat{6}$ for $\hat{4}$" technique discussed in the text.

For the development: The lowest note of the left hand clarifies the role of the dominant throughout this brief development section. In dominant prolongations, the upper voice often moves through one or more intervals of the underlying V. Discover the interval here by tracing the stepwise line in bars 27–31, beginning on g^1. If d^2 is still active at a deeper level, what technique does the stepwise line represent?

For the recapitulation: The recapitulation in Clementi's Sonatina is a relatively straightforward reworking of the exposition. Prepare *two* graphs as you did for the exposition. Now, of course, the second sketch will also illustrate a tonic prolongation. Consider how the two main upper-voice motions (one for each section) function within the *Urlinie* of the entire compositions. Give special consideration to the role of the linear progression of the second theme (bars 49–82). What structural motion does it represent in the recapitulation?

The corresponding transition section of a recapitulation is often where the modification (of the exposition) becomes clear. Show in your graph Clementi's changes, which "prevent" a modulation to V, and maintain the global tonic of C major. Hint: Clementi underscores this pivotal area with a crescendo from *piano* to *fortissimo* in bars 40–44. Finally, compare the relationship between form and structure in this movement to that of Mozart's Trio analyzed in Assignment No. 34.

Assignment 40

Spiritoso.

Assignment 40

Assignment 40

Assignment 40

Assignment No. 41 Mozart, String Quartet, K. 172, Adagio (Chapter 11)

This piece goes "just beyond" a rounded binary; because of the characteristics of bars 19–31 (the conclusion of the movement), this section can be considered a legitimate recapitulation. Hence, the composition is a slow-movement sonata form. Use the instructions given for the previous assignment, including dividing the exposition (and recapitulation) into two sections as you analyze. Refer to the discussion of the "Haffner" symphony in the text.

For the exposition: Mozart doesn't actually "modulate" to V, rather just uses the half cadence of bar 4 as the method of establishing B♭ major (this kind of motion is typical of his style). The midpoint of the exposition is at bar 5; consider bars 5ff. to be in the dominant, with its own (local) *Urlinie*. The chord in bar 9 is II$^6_5$ in the dominant; you will need to consider whether C or E♭ is the main tone in the upper voice. Important: The cello line in bar 11 suggests two registers and hence a bass and a tenor voice; this observation will prove useful for the analysis of the development section.

For the development section: Does the E♭-major chord in bar 12 represent a return to tonic harmony, or could the bass perhaps belong to the "tenor" voice mentioned earlier? Consider the ramifications of both. In a general sense, the goal of a development in the major mode is usually V; in this piece, the dominant appears in bars 17–18. Compare carefully the first V in bar 17 with the chord on the fourth beat of bar 18. What technique does Mozart use to "prepare" the beginning of the recapitulation? Refer to Example 11.11 in the text to help you answer this question.

For the recapitulation: The first part (bars 19–22) is literally restated from the exposition. The second part (bars 23–30) appears now in the tonic (a standard technique of sonata form). The question is this: How does one determine the function of the local structural melody (now in E♭ major) to the *Urlinie* of the composition? Use Example 12.11 in the text as your guide.

Assignment 41

Assignment 41

Assignment 41

Assignment 41

Assignment 41